That Time I Was Committed

Kaylee Segar

For my son, Brighton. You were <u>still</u> born.

It had been 10 days since I was committed to the mental hospital for a suicide attempt. There were many things leading up to this event, but you'll have to read another one of my books to find out about them. During my stay at the hospital, I grew comfortable with myself, my thoughts, and the words that I would start writing in the journal the therapist gave me. I learned a lot and I wrote a lot. When I was released my husband bought me a pink leather journal so I could keep up with my therapeutic outlet and the peace that had found me. Some days I would write about things that bothered me and then they would turn into rhymes that started to flow out of my brain and onto the pages of my journal. I have always been an unknown blogger of sorts, so when I started to post my poems on my blog and noticed they were getting attention, especially from the mental illness community, I decided to compile my favorites into a book. I've considered trying to become a writer for the past couple of years but never really tried to make it happen. While the idea of becoming a published writer was floating around in my head, the words of many motivational speakers I had been listening to replayed repeatedly in my mind throughout the days and I finally got off my ass and then sat it down at my desk to create this project.

I like to think of this book as lyrics for an album that doesn't exist. I'm not a singer or a song writer, but I did enjoy pouring my heart and mind onto these pages. Writing has always been an outlet for me but I've always compared myself to other authors. When I realized that I don't have to be like everyone else or even follow all the rules, I felt inspired.

1. I Don't Care

Flipping through all these pages
Of words that I've written
About my life, my love,
And the diagnosis I've been given

I've learned I don't care
About any of it at all
I don't care about their problems
I don't care if they all collapse and
fall

I don't care that I was
manipulated
50 times over
I don't care that I'm a different
Fucking person when I'm sober

I don't care if they hate my guts,
Or they call me a slut, or say that
it's just my luck
And I don't care that they don't
know the truth
They don't know what didn't
really happen
Between me and you

You- who I'm not talking to, not
writing to
Because you don't matter, you
aren't real
You- who played the game better
than anyone
But now how does it feel
To be on your own now,
With no one to have your back this
time

Like you didn't have mine
When I swore I wasn't lying
And you screamed in my face
And you helped him get mad
And I defended myself and i cried
But neither one of you could look past
The place we were all in, the mind frame you chose
I won't out you now, because it'll ruin you both

So I took the pills and I swallowed them all
And I was ready to end it because you started it all
But I survived and I'm alive and I'll never do it again

And I won't trust you one more
time,
Even if you swear you're my
friend

I can't care about what we said
when
We felt mad or sad or hurt so bad
I can't care because I'm breathing
now
And it's not about everything i
once had

It's about this moment right here
Feeling the cool breeze on my nose,
cheeks, and ears
And about finishing one thing at a
time

So I don't lose my goddamn
freaking mind

I don't care if you tell me I should
try harder to kill myself next time
I don't care if you apologize and
come to me begging and crying
I don't care about your words or
your threats followed by your
promises to be better
I can't care about you
Because I have to care about ME
getting better

2. The Attractive Spider

You're a spider, but an attractive
one
And you know the things you're
capable of
You don't love 'em and leave 'em
You tease them and bring them
Along with you on your fantasy
ride
They don't know the truth, or
where they're going,
But they've got you by their side

But who are you? the Joker?
So special when you're sober
But your face lies every time you
blink your eyes

Have girls staying up all night,
Have people ruining their lives

You're a monster, but a good one
And we all had a good run

But you turn your back quick
And pull the strings, making
everyone trip
And then you leave us behind
Choking in the smoke left from
your fires

Were we in your web the whole
time?

Chapter 3. Slow Dance

Paxil at night to help with my
mind
Trazadone to dance with it,
helping me sleep tight
Klonopin during the day,
whenever I feel anxious
Vistaril for backup, when I really
just can't take it

I lose my patience
I lose my sanity
I want to be normal
But not sure what's left of me

I have to be vulnerable. I have to
let them see
Even if it's possible that I don't

know the real me
Am I embarrassed or ashamed to
be naked on these pages?
Am I okay, am I reaching out?
Am I just going trough more
phases?

Paxil at night helps ease my mind
Trazadone slow dances me to
sleep
Klonopin periodically to mellow
me out
Vistaril when the whole damn
world seems too loud
My journal for times when I just
can't figure it out

Chapter 4. Mindfully

I wish I wasn't judged for taking a
nap
I'm not depressed; my brain just
feels attacked
I want to stay in a euphoric zone
I don't think I wanna be alone
But this house is my home and the
tension, it grows,
And my bones feel so weak
I just want to fucking sleep

I'm not depressed, my brain is just
stressed
I'm not lying or hiding or crying
to myself
I'm not wishing I was dying or
harming myself

It's just so loud in here
Why can't you all be still?

Is that question selfish because
that's really how I felt it
and I'm still wondering if you
will...

Just be still...

Just sit with me quietly
Let me close my eyes mindfully
Let me erase my aches and ease
my pain
Can you just breathe right beside
me
Can we just sit here quietly?

Chapter 5. Stillborn

It's going to take Mommy a few
tries to write this poem
I want it to be real and if
somehow you can hear or feel
I just want you to know this

I regret when I cried because I
found out you were a boy
I'm the shittiest mom – I should've
been overjoyed
I regret the day I didn't go to the
doctor sooner
You must've been struggling,
begging me to hear you

I'm sorry I let you die
I'm sorry I barely tried

To eat right, to exercise, to
protect my mind From all the
fights

I'm sorry i couldn't save you, fuck
I didn't even get to bathe you once
When they let me hold you,
I feel like I gave up too soon
I'd give anything to be back in
that hospital room

Brighton, you were loved, so loved
You were born breaking hearts
People ruined our time together
And now we'll always be apart

I hope my medicine keeps me
from crying
I hope the tears don't well up

because
Once they start pouring,
There's no damn point in trying

If magic is real, if prayer is real
If wishes came true, you know I'd
pick you
I'd do anything, anything at all
To see what color your eyes were
I'd do anything, anything in the
world
To have seen your beautiful smile

Brighton baby, I'm sorry.
I'm sorry I can't be your mommy
I'm sorry that everything went so
wrong
I hope i did good
I hope you were happy

I hope at least I kept you a little
bit warm

Brighton, my best and hardest
day
was the day you were born

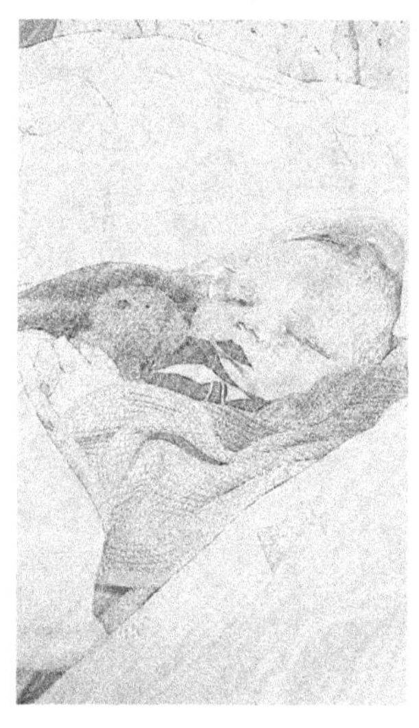

Chapter 6. Point of View

I swear there used to
be **butterflies**
And not a goddamned person
Who could tell me **otherwise**
And I've tried my hardest
to **explain**
That some things about me will
just never be the **same**

I carried him, I mothered him
I felt him kick my **stomach**
Now it just feels like there's
a **hole** in my **stomach**,
Like somebody **punched it**
and they took my heart and
ran **off with it**,
And they **lost it**
And they're so sorry but

no **cost can fix**
The **loss of him**
Because *I* lost him
I go to sleep at night and wake up
from this Same **dream** again
It's on **repeat** again
Just let me **breathe** again

And sometimes I cry
But I can't let you **see**
Because you always seem to get so
worried about **me**

And sometimes it hurts so bad
that I **bleed** on the inside,
I **grieve** on the inside
I fought all I can **fight**
I can never make it **right**
I can never bring him **back**

This is all of me that I **have**

There's nothing left of **me**
Not enough for **you**
I'm not trying to be **free**
Just want you to see my point
of **view**

Chapter 7. If I Show You My Journal

When I hold you it feels
Like a campfire warming my soul
when you laugh I feel proud
Because it was a joke that I told
When we shower and I scrub your
back
And I see your freckles and
tattoos
I smile because I'm madly in love
with you

I'm afraid if I show you my journal
you'll yell
You'll say I don't love you
You'll swear you can tell
That's not true, Love
It's not what I mean
Because out of all I have,

You're the the thing I need

If I can't open up to you
Then what do you suggest I do
If I can't let you in my soul
Will you eventually decide to go?

I'm trying to be me and hoping
that you'll see
You inspire every dream
you encourage every leap
I just need you to believe

Chapter 8. I'm So Hot

It's 40 degrees out and I'm in a
tank top,
Sitting on the back porch,
Writing, trying to make it stop
I'm so hot

It's like every thought floods
through my mind
At the same time
And I start to sweat
But I can't stop yet
I have to make you proud,
Have to make you see
That I'm doing everything I can
So you'll believe in me
But I'm so hot
I can't breathe in this house

I'm stuck
I can't leave your grasp,
I must
Fulfill my vows,
I must
Make it work somehow
I must
Be a better wife,
Like i was
When we look back on time

Is there any getting passed all of it
Will a band-aid just fall right off
of it

Look how long we've lasted but all
our wheels have fallen off, make it
stop
The bolts have been messed with

Your head, you don't understand
it
And I'm so hot

I'm just so hot trying to figure this
out
Trying to get through this
drought
We can't reach our potential if
we're just walking around
Bumping into each other and
then falling back down
So I'm sitting outside
In the winter time
Wearing no sleeves 'cause
I can't fucking breathe
And I'm so hot

Chapter 9. A Simple Task

I wish I could be
normal
I wish simple things
didn't scare me
When you ask me to do
something easy
And it feels like you
triple dog dared me

What you need is
someone
Who can take a little
drive into town I
Without popping an
anxiety pill
What you deserve is
someone

Who doesn't over think
everything
To the point of being
afraid
Their every thought is
going to spill

Out onto the floor
Now I'm embarrassed
So damn insecure
I can never just walk
into a room
And feel 100% sure
Of myself, of my
health,
Of my ability to
control my breath

Now I'm weirdly
aware of how loudly
I'm Breathing
And how fast my
heart is actually
Beating
And now my sweat is
streaming
From my forehead to
my back
And my stomach is all
twisted and out of
whack
All because you asked
me my favorite hobby

What is a hobby?
You do things for fun?
You have time in

between sleeping and
worrying to go for a
run?
To enjoy something
more, to have a
passion, A desire, the
ability to adore?

You know, my brain is
a puzzle
That I've lost all the
pieces to
And I can't keep my
voice steady
Long enough to speak
it through

You know, that's the
reason I get so

paranoid
I'm never enjoying, I'm
always outpouring,
Out-crying for help or
attention
And all the other crazy
pieces I can't even
mention

I'm afraid of standing
still
Because if you look at
me to long you'll get a
fill
You'll get full of my
annoyances,
My bad habits I can't
break
Everyone gets sick of

my anxiety
My uncertainty they
can't take

I get mad when you
ask me to run to the
store
Not because I don't
want to help
But it's so, so much
more

I don't know where I'm
going
I don't know which
side of the road to be
on
I feel like I'm lonely so I
turn the radio on

And scream along
And I'm lost in the car
And in my head
I'm alive
But I'm constantly
consumed with dread

Chapter 10. Leave

One minute I'm flying
high on fantasy and
imagination
The next second I'm
chasing you without a
thought, without any
hesitation

It doesn't make sense,
the toying around and
stringing me up just to
throw me back down

It's convenient that
they all run away
After promising,
swearing, making me

believe they'll really
stay

Sometimes it's
without a trace
Sometimes it's so fast
Not a single minute
left to waste
On me and my
carefree thoughts
My only desire being to
watch
You walk and talk and
breathe in my
direction
and so I reach out too
much and I show too
much affection

And I drink and I cry
And then another
week and some
months go by
And I finally fall asleep,
accepting defeat
Accepting the fact
that you really did
leave

Chapter 11. Cease and Desist

Why? Why do you find
reasons to hate me
and make me
unwanted?
Why? Why do you spin
and twist and turn
things around
until every night I'm
haunted?
Are you? Are you
happy stirring fire,
making me bleed,
wishing I'd died?
Do you? Do you
understand reality or
is it a fun, painful

fantasy you desire?

I've tried so hard to
understand
I've cried, we've
laughed, you held my
hand
But you hate me and
you enjoy it
nothing I'll ever say
can destroy it

so I'm saying goodbye
the best way I know
how
I'm not going to try –
you can't talk to me
now

Chapter 12. Okay

Have you ever been too tired to
take a shower
I'm not talking about when
depression takes over your every
waking hour
I'm talking about being exhausted
from accomplishing so much and
you feel empowered

Have you ever laid down and not
felt guilty for looking lazy
Because you know today you
fought the urge to give into your
crazy

It feels right to sip cheap wine
even though I shouldn't on my

medication
I feel like I'm enough and I fought
all anxiety's goddamn
temptation
I was strong today I
 was queen today
Nothing was wrong today
And today was okay

Have you ever felt a drip of sweat
on your forehead
Not from being nervous, but from
being proactive
Have you ever felt like it was
alright to smile
Like you made it to the end of all
those all those back
breaking fucking miles

It feels right to sip cheap wine
even though I shouldn't on my
medication
I feel like I'm enough and I fought
all anxiety's goddamn
temptation
I was strong today
I was queen today
Nothing was wrong today
And today was okay